Dr. Katie Canty   Introduction to Computer Keyboarding   1 to 2-Week

Computer Keyboarding
Basic Training Camp for Hunt & Peckers and Beginners

beyondcomputerbasics@yahoo.com   seniortechacademy@yahoo.com

ISBN-13: 978-1975797683

ISBN-10: 197579768X

copyright 2017 Dr. Katie Canty, Ed. D.

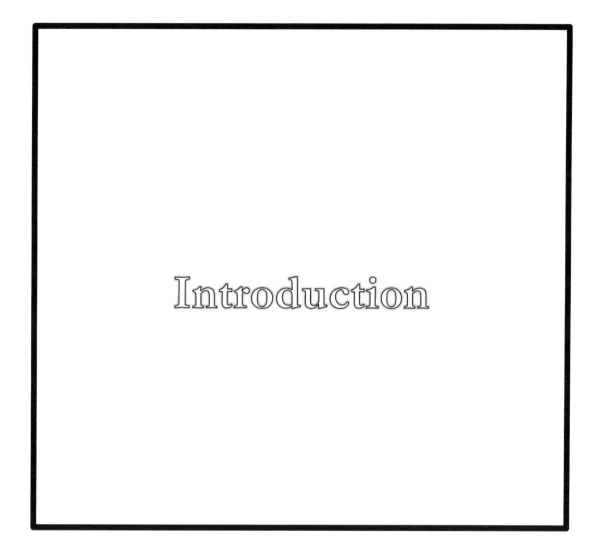

If you hunt and peck, or if you want to type with all ten fingers, this introductory computer keyboarding course is for you. One of the first steps in learning how to use a home or office computer is learning how to type with all ten fingers on a computer keyboard.

Let's begin to type right with Dr. Canty as your typing teacher and coach plus goodtyping.com as your online classroom.

- Each student keys ten lessons. Each lesson may take 10 to 20 minutes to type.
- Upon completion of all ten lessons, earn a printable certificate with your highest speed and accuracy score noted.

The goals of this introductory keyboarding course are:

1. good keyboarding techniques

2. familiarity with home row, top, and bottom keyboard key locations

3. correctly keying of capital letters and punctuation marks

4. keyboard navigation skill building

5. speed and accuracy skill building

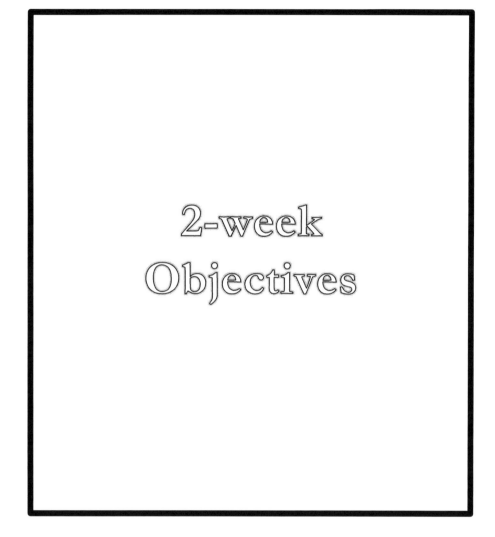

Week 1

- Good keyboarding techniques
- Keyboarding terms
- Lesson completion suggestions
- Online Lessons 1-5

Week 2

- Lessons 6-10
- More Keyboarding terms
- Skill assessment and certificate

Let's Begin

just 5 steps

Step 1

Good keyboarding techniques video

Let's get started typing right. Look at this You-tube Video First.

https://www.youtube.com/watch?v=8Ic2L7ZyFC8

Keyboarding Quiz

1. What are the home row keys?

2. According to the YouTube video, what is one of the best techniques for learning to type well?

3. What keys are used to make a letter a capital letter?

Step 2

Enter our online keyboarding practice website.

- Go to www.goodtyping.com.
- Look for the LOG IN tab.
- Enter an email address and the password that you want to use for the duration of the course.

3 Tips for Avoiding software malfunction

Tip 1 - CAPS LOCK KEY: If the keyboarding classroom software locks up while you are typing, press the CAPS LOCK key to unlock the software. On some computers, a light shows up next to the caps lock key when it is on. If you press the caps Lock key again, this will start things back working. The caps lock key is a TOGGLE key, which means you press it to turn it on and press it again to turn it off.

Tip 2 - RED LINE: This means the keyboard letter needs to be typed in order to move on.

Tip 3 - END OF LINE: Press the ENTER key to move to a new line.

Step 3

Key Lessons 1-5.

Lesson Completion Suggestions

Suggestion 1 - LESSON COMPLETION: Complete all the lines in each lesson. If a few lines or half a lesson is completed, the software will not save it as a completed lesson. It usually takes 15 to 18 minutes for a beginner to complete a lesson.

Suggestion 2 – CAMP DURATION: Try to complete one lesson per day. This way you can finish in two weeks or less.

Suggestion 3 - REPEAT OR GO TO NEXT LESSON: Yes, a lesson can be repeated several times. If you are backspacing a lot to correct errors, this is a good indication that a lesson needs to be rekeyed before going on to the next lesson.

Three Computer Keyboarding Terms

1. Keyboarding - means the same thing as typing but usually refers to typing on a computer keyboard rather than a manual typewriter

2. Shift Keys - used to make capital letters; one located on the right and one located on the left side of the keyboard--Press the shift key and then the letter you want to make a capital letter. Let go of the shift key and continue with regular case keying.

3. Text Wrapping - no need to press the ENTER key-- text automatically goes to the next line as when taking a typing timed writing test

Step 4

Keyboarding Lessons 6-10

Speed and Accuracy Goals - Desirable Words Per Minute (WPM

Category		Range (WPM)	Mean (WPM)
Kids	Very Slow	<11	-
	Slow	11 - 20	15
	Average	21 - 30	25
	Fast	31 - 40	35
	Very Fast	>40	-
Adults	Very Slow	<26	-
	Slow/Beginner	26 - 35	30
	Intermediate/Average	36 - 45	40
	Fast/Advanced	46 - 65	55
	Very Fast	66 - 80	73
	Insane	>80	-
	Fastest in The World	-	216*
Jobs	Entry Level Clerk/Secretary	35 - 60	-
	Higher/Advanced Level Clerk/Secretary	60 - 80	-
	Data Entry	60 - 80	-
	Dispatch Position/Time Sensitive	80 - 95	-

Three More Computer Keyboarding Terms

1. Timed Writing - Measures typing speed and accuracy

2. Semi-colon and Colon - Punctuation marks across from the L key: Press the shift key to make a colon. Key the semicolon with the smaller pinky finger on the right hand.

3. Period - Punctuation mark at the end of a sentence: Space 1 time after keying a period between sentences.

Step 5

Skill Assessment & Your Certificate

- Go to goodtyping.com.
- Select the Typing Speed Test Tab.
- Take at least 2 timed writings.
- Print a certificate for your best-timed writing.
- Let us know how well you did by commenting at TpT, Tech Seekers.

Typing tips and techniques

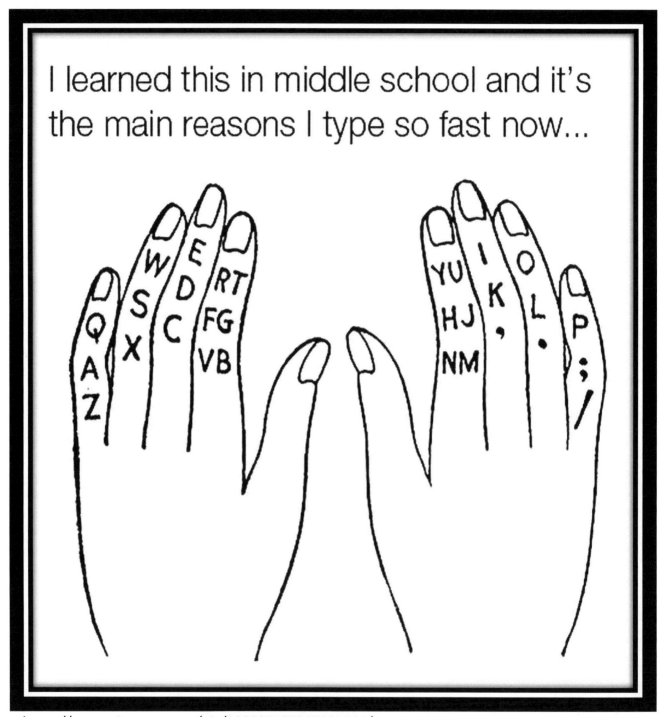

https://www.pinterest.com/pin/108227197277802731/

Typing tips, how to make type faster and master the keyboard

https://www.keyhero.com/wpm-typing-tips/?page=3&lang=0

notcrowley

My tip to improve your typing speed is to... read the quote and type. Do not type fast if you are not fully familiar with the keys.

Reply

arjun007

What really helped me improve my typing speed is... only and only daily a night practice of typing. it improves your movement of your fingers

hop.holly

My tip to beginners to is not look down at the keys when you start because then it will become a habit and even when you know where the keys are you will still be looking down at the keyboard.

leggo

My tip to improve your typing speed is to…

Continue to type as much as possible. If you find yourself lacking on a certain key, find some practice on that key. I personally do a little worse when I'm constantly shifting for the lower left side of my keyboard, and I'm working on that. After you know roughly what you're doing, practice without looking and build up via accuracy, and not speed. Remember that last part always.

ryanart

Don't look at the keyboard. If you see you made a mistake, press the backspace and try again. You won't learn anything by sticking to the same thing you've always done.

diamonds

My tip to improve your typing speed is to… always look at the keyboard before typing so that you can know what keys to press while trying not to look at the keyboard while typing. Good luck.

protostar 7 months, 1 week ago

What really helped me improve my typing speed is...spending time each night just 3 or 4 round of the typing test has improved my accuracy and speed exponentially I started not knowing how to type with all my fingers but knew where the letters were well I didn't really know which fingers to hit each key with but using this test and a lil practice I have jumped from 4wpm to nearly 16wpm with 4 or 5 days of practice

firefingers1992 3 weeks, 5 days ago

Hey user72299, sorry this reply took so long. Here are some tips on how you can get to at least 100 wpm: Practice for at least 4 days per week, 1.5 hours per day. If you need to, you can even type for 45 minutes (with drinking water now and then, really quick), and then come back to it with 45 minutes again. Also, practice the piano. That will help.

layle 4 months, 4 weeks ago

What really helped me improve my typing speed is... keeping your posture. Always keep your hands in the normal layout that is supposed to be, pinky on a, ring on s, middle on d, and pointer on f, for your left hand. Do the same for the other hand but keep the pointer on J and just let the rest of your fingers minus the thumb on the keys after J. Aka, J K L and; Depending on if you're left or right handed, you'll end up pressing space with your right or left hand. Me, being left handed, I end up finding myself pressing space with my left thumb and keeping my right hand a bit more spread out.

rapidtyping.com

wirecutter.com

Typing/Computer Keyboarding Practice Sessions Diary

Name _____

Lesson #	Completion Date	Start time	Finish time	Notes
1				
2				
3				
4				
5				
6				
7				
8				
9				
10				

beyondcomputerbasics@yahoo.com   seniortechacademy@yahoo.com

Typing/Computer Keyboarding
Speed & Accuracy Timed Writings Practice Tests

Name _____

3-minute timed writings		
Date of Test	Words Per Minute	Errors

5-minute timed writings		
Date of Test	Words Per Minute	Errors

Your Typing/Computer Keyboarding Certificate

Print out a hard copy of your certificate. Be sure to scan and save an image of your typing certificate, too.

Insert or place the image here.

ABOUT THE AUTHOR

Dr. Canty is on a collaborative mission to spread computer technology literacy among multi-generational populations in every county and country--1 byte at a time.

Made in the USA
Columbia, SC
14 October 2020